MW00636373

better together*

*This book is best read together, grownup and kid.

akidsco.com

a
kids
book
about

a kids book about PUBERTY

by Dr. Heather Chow

a
kids
book
about

Printed in the United States of America.

A Kids Book About books are available online: *akidsco.com*

To share your stories, ask questions, or inquire about bulk purchases (schools, libraries, and nonprofits), please use the following email address: *hello@akidsco.com*

Hardback ISBN: 978-1-958825-53-2
Ebook ISBN: 978-1-958825-54-9

Designed by Rick DeLucco
Edited by Emma Wolf

To all the people in my life who inspire me—
my husband, my sister and brother, my parents
and in-laws, my mentors, and my patients.

But especially to past Heather going through
puberty—a bright-eyed, often awkward,
pigtail-wearing late bloomer.

You might be hesitant to talk about puberty with your kid. Maybe all you remember are the really embarrassing parts, like finding your first armpit hair or getting teased about acne.

This book is here to remind you that puberty is a universal occurrence. All grownups have gone through it, and it's a healthy part of growing up. Puberty is also a sensory experience, and we'll explore changes we can see, feel, hear, and—let's be honest—smell.

But, just like everybody is unique, every *body* experiences puberty differently. These changes can differ from person to person and within oneself too!

Ultimately, puberty shouldn't be a mystery. Kids shouldn't be left on their own to navigate the physical and emotional complexities of this transition from childhood to adulthood. I hope this book provides the opportunity for you and your kiddos to ask questions openly and share personal stories, no matter how embarrassing they may seem.

Let's say this word together: **puberty.**

(PEW-BURH-TEE...

PUBERTY!

GOOD JOB!

Puberty can feel like a weird thing to talk about. But I'm excited for this important conversation. Are you?

SO, WHAT IS PUBERTY?

It’s a time when a lot of change happens—your body will change and you will experience more emotions.

When people talk about **puberty**, they sometimes use words that sound funny, or use a different word in place of the real thing.

That's because grownups aren't always comfortable talking about **puberty**.

But I'm going to use the real names because it's really important.*

*For a list of words used throughout the book and their meanings, check out the glossary in the back!

Puberty is a completely normal part of growing up.

All grownups have gone through puberty, including...

YOUR PARENTS.

YOUR AUNTS *and* UNCLES.

YOUR GRANDPARENTS.

YOUR TEACHERS.

YOUR DOCTORS.

YOUR COACHES.

EVEN ME.

Hi! MY NAME IS HEATHER.

I am a pediatrician, which means I'm a doctor for kids.

I'm a grownup now, but I
still remember what it was like
when I went through **puberty**.

I felt awkward, embarrassed, and didn't think I could openly talk about it with my grownups.

Maybe you feel the same way

(AND THAT'S OK!).

I hope to answer some questions you may have and share ways that **puberty** can be easier to talk about.

ALRIGHT, LET'S DO THIS!

Puberty is driven by 2 main hormones*:

TESTOSTERONE *and* ESTROGEN.

*Hormones are chemical messengers your body produces that affect different processes in your body over time.

Humans have different balances of these 2 hormones. Estrogen mainly causes changes in kids with a vagina while testosterone drives change primarily in kids with a penis.

These hormones tell your body what to do during **puberty**. Some of these changes are external and easy to see, while others are internal and not as obvious.

- TESTOSTERONE TELLS THE PENIS *and* TESTICLES TO GROW.
- ESTROGEN TELLS THE BREASTS TO DEVELOP.
- TESTOSTERONE TELLS YOUR MUSCLES TO GET STRONGER.
- ESTROGEN TELLS THE BODY TO MENSTRUATE.
- TESTOSTERONE TELLS THE TESTICLES TO MAKE SPERM.
- ESTROGEN *and* TESTOSTERONE TELL YOUR BODY TO GROW TALLER.

Every body will experience **puberty** differently. You may notice some of these changes, or different versions of them, but whatever you experience is a normal part of growing up.

YOU'VE GOT THIS!

You already went through tons of changes as a baby becoming a kid. And **puberty** is just another stage of growth toward becoming a young adult.

As I mentioned before,
some changes are going
to be pretty easy to see.

Like body hair, which grows
everywhere and in places
you maybe didn't think
could grow hair!

You also may notice acne on your face, back, chest, or other places on your body.

Developing acne doesn't mean you're not cleaning yourself well enough—it's your hormones doing their work!

Your sleeves and pant legs might seem shorter and your shoes may feel tighter. Growth spurts are a normal part of **puberty** too.

Puberty can also get a bit

You may notice new odor coming from your armpits or genital area. It's also normal to sweat more!

You may also *hear* some changes as your body goes through **puberty**. When our bodies produce testosterone, we may notice some cracking in our voice while speaking, or that our voice gets deeper.

THESE THINGS ARE
USUALLY OBVIOUS.

BUT SOME CHANGES
AREN'T SO NOTICEABLE.

Puberty can be confusing.
You might have strong emotions
you haven't experienced before,
and you might not understand
why you're feeling them.
That's SO frustrating, right?

I remember feeling very impatient, irritable, or even aggressive toward my loved ones. Other feelings could include embarrassment, sexual attraction, or the need for privacy.

During **puberty**, your hormones are working to find a balance, but sometimes it takes a while. All of this happens on a timeline outside of your control, and every body's timeline is different.

It can be easy to compare your experience with that of your friends or classmates. Know that whatever you are seeing, smelling, hearing, or feeling is normal.*

*If you have questions or feel confused, or are worried about any of the changes you notice, I encourage you to talk to a trusted grownup.

PHEW!

That was a lot of stuff. How are you feeling? If you have questions already, feel free to pause and talk to your grownup about them. When you're ready to keep going, turn the page.

As a doctor, I get a lot of questions from kids and grownups about **puberty**. They wonder whether these changes are normal, because some may be unexpected.

- ONE TESTICLE MIGHT GROW BIGGER THAN THE OTHER.
- ONE BREAST MAY BE SMALLER.
- BREAST DEVELOPMENT CAN HAPPEN IN KIDS WITH A VAGINA *and* IN KIDS WITH A PENIS.
- THE RIGHT SIDE OF YOUR VULVA MIGHT LOOK DIFFERENT FROM THE LEFT SIDE.
- ERECTIONS CAN HAPPEN UNEXPECTEDLY.
- YOU MIGHT EVEN EXPERIENCE SOMETHING CALLED WET DREAMS.

For those with a penis, **puberty** will be the first time that semen—a usually white sticky substance or liquid—comes out of the penis. Some kids can tell this is about to happen when the penis becomes engorged and gets harder.

Unfortunately, this can happen when we least expect it, like while we are sleeping (that's what I mean by wet dreams).

This might feel embarrassing, but nocturnal emissions are a normal part of **puberty**.

Some events in **puberty** happen in cycles. For kids with a vagina, that includes menstruation (commonly called a period).

This is when the uterine lining sheds and comes out of the vagina once a month. It's part of a bigger reproduction cycle.

PERIODS CAN FEEL LIKE A BIG CHANGE IN YOUR BODY, BUT **DON'T WORRY**. YOUR BODY IS EQUIPPED TO DO IT.

There's a wide range of experiences that can come with having a period. Like...

STOMACH CRAMPING OR DISCOMFORT, BACK PAIN, HEADACHES,

OR FEELING SADNESS,
ANGER, IMPATIENCE,
JOY, OR IRRITATION.

Everyone's period is different, so there are different products to help you manage it. The most important thing is that you find what brings you **comfort.**

Pads, tampons, absorbent underwear, or menstrual cups absorb or catch period blood. Try them out to find what works best for your body!

This has been a **LOT** of information. It's **OK** if you're feeling overwhelmed, totally confident about puberty, or somewhere in between.

REMEMBER, YOU ARE NOT ALONE.

Every human goes through **puberty.**

ALL OF THESE CHANGES ARE NORMAL. AND IT'S IMPORTANT TO TALK ABOUT OUR BODIES.

Conversations about **puberty**
don't have to be uncomfortable.

It’s also **SUPER** important to spend time getting to know your body and understand the changes it’s experiencing.

Familiarizing yourself with how your body uniquely goes through **puberty** can help you recognize changes, ask questions, and get the support you need to feel awesome.

You did it!

Puberty is pretty amazing,

AND SO ARE YOU!

Going through puberty can be a confusing time for your kid and for you. But hopefully now you feel more prepared to support your kiddo during this important transition.

Here are a few ways you can break the ice when it comes to puberty:

Share your own stories to help them feel comfortable expressing their concerns. Remind your kid that these changes are normal and that puberty's a normal part of growing up.

Ask, *What changes do you think about the most?* Reassure them that after puberty, even though they'll look, sound, feel, and smell different, underneath it all, they are still themselves!

Ask, *What are you feeling right now?* Sometimes kids want more privacy and may need time to open up. That's totally OK. Give them space and let them know that when they're ready, you'll be there to listen.

If you or your kid are worried about certain changes, feel free to ask your kid's pediatrician. We're always here to help.

About The Author

Dr. Heather Chow (she/her) takes care of kiddos from birth to 18 years old, watching them grow and supporting them through all of their physical and emotional changes. From her many interactions with kids and their grownups, she knows people have a lot of questions about puberty.

As a kid, Dr. Chow felt overwhelmed by the exciting, yet unfamiliar, changes happening to her body. She remembers feeling alone, unsure of who she could talk to or confide in. However, this uncomfortable feeling dissipated upon realizing she could share her concerns with her pediatrician.

Since then, she's carried with her the belief that sharing personal stories about puberty helps kids realize that they are not alone in what they're experiencing. With this book, she hopes to go beyond the walls of her clinic to extend these important conversations between kids and their grownups everywhere. Additionally, Dr. Chow wishes to empower kids to be experts of their own bodies.

 @drheatherchow

Glossary

Acne: small, usually red, white, or yellow bumps filled with oil and skin cells, also known as pimples

Breast: soft tissue which forms a mound of varying sizes on the chest area

Egg: a specialized reproductive cell that is tiny and round; produced in the ovaries

Erection: hardening and enlargement of the penis because of increased blood flow to the area

Estrogen: a hormone made in the ovaries and testicles that tells different parts of the body what to do

Genitals: the reproductive organs that are located externally on the body, such as a penis or a vulva; also referred to as genitalia or private parts

Ovary: an oval-shaped organ located in the abdomen which makes and stores eggs and produces hormones such as estrogen; there are usually 2 ovaries, 1 located on each side of the uterus

Menstruate: to have a period; when our bodies shed the lining of our uterus monthly due to a hormone-driven process. A period can include blood, human body tissue, and other fluids

Penis: a genital organ located between the legs that urine and semen comes out of

Semen: a sticky white fluid made of sperm, proteins, and sugar that comes out of the penis

Sexual Attraction: strong emotional interest or desire toward another person

Sperm: a specialized reproductive cell with a tail to help it move; produced in the testicles

Testicle: an oval-shaped organ located within a skin sac called the scrotum that hangs behind the penis; sperm is made here

Testosterone: a hormone made in the testicles and ovaries that tells different parts of the body what to do

Vagina: a muscular canal that connects the outside genital area to the uterus, which is located in the body's pelvic area for those with a vagina

Vulva: the outer part of the genitals that includes the vagina's opening, fleshy skin folds called labia majora (outer skin folds) and labia minora (inner skin folds), and the clitoris (a sensitive area of the genitals located above the labia minora)

a
kids
book
about
SAFETY
by Soraya Sutherlin, CEM

a
kids
book
about
IMAGINATION
by LEVAR BURTON

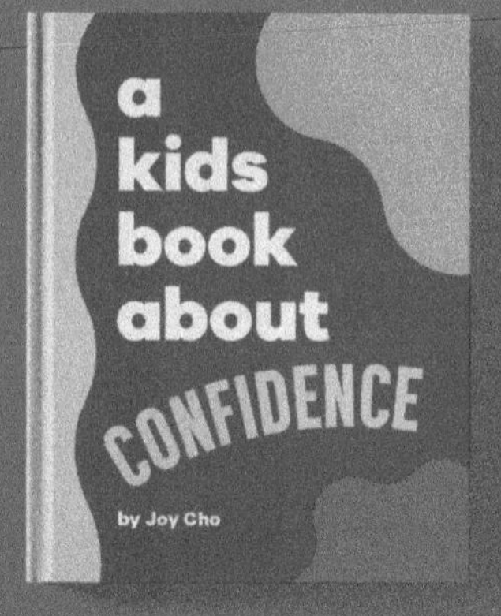

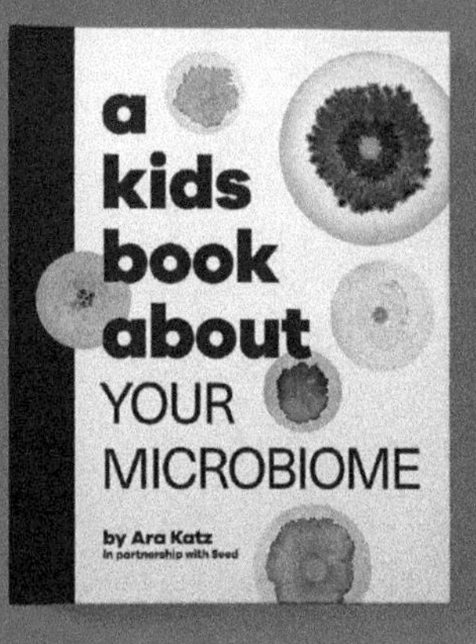

Discover more
at akidsco.com